DESIGN YOUR THRIVE

Your Path | Your Purpose | Your Journey

CAREER CROSSROADS
EDITION

Julie Jones, MS, RDN, LD, CPTD

"My mission in life is not merely to survive,
but to **THRIVE;**
and to do so with some passion,
some compassion, some humor,
and some style."

\- Maya Angelou -

ISBN: 979-8-35097-758-5
BookBaby Publishing, 2024

TABLE OF CONTENTS

01 | INTRODUCTION

Introduction	05
Career Crossroads Examples	06-07
Tenets of Design Your **THRIVE**	08-09

02 | INTENTION

Intention Introduction	12-13
Assessment Exercises	14-17
Reflection & Notes	18-22

03 | TRUST & RELATIONSHIPS

Trust & Relationships Introduction	24-25
Assessment Exercises	26-31
Summary Reflection & Notes	32-34

04 | GROWTH & DEVELOPMENT

Growth & Development Intro	36-37
Assessment Exercises	38-43
Knowledge, Behaviors, Skills Definitions	44-47
Reflection & Notes	48-50

05 | CAREER EXPLORATION

Career Exploration Learning	52-55
Reflection Activities	56-57
Career Exploration Planning	58-60

06 | SUMMARY ROAD MAP

Design Your THRIVE Road Map	61
Summary Reflection	62-64
DYT Development Plan	65-68
DYT Progress Update	69-70
Shift Into Drive	71

ARE YOU AT A JOB OR CAREER CROSSROADS?

At some point in your work life, you encounter pivotal moments that define your path - career crossroads. These are stages where you may feel stuck, desire growth, experience burnout, or seek to pivot towards something new. Whether you're evaluating your current state of **THRIVE** at work, seeking mentorship and guidance for your next steps, embarking on a new job, or gaining a new leader, these moments are opportunities for reflection, evaluation, and decision-making.

Design Your THRIVE is your compass at these critical points, helping you claim or reclaim your thrive at work or in your career —navigating not just your job but your path, purpose, and journey. Our approach taps into intention, relationships, trust, and learning to help you navigate these crossroads successfully.

You are the driver of your career vehicle. The roadmap for your journey is grounded in **intention**, your travel partners are informed by **trust & relationships; growth & development** are the GPS adjustments. How does the driver - YOU - and the roadmap evolve and change through your journey?

As you stand at the intersection of stay, go, or grow in your current role or embark on a new chapter, ***Design Your THRIVE*** equips you with the tools to provide direction and support as you compile your road map.

YOU'RE NOT ALONE

More people are facing career crossroads than at any other time in recent decades. According to the Gallup organization, only one-third of U.S. employees were engaged in their work, with more than 50% either struggling or suffering at work (2022). Leadership turnover, layoffs, return-to-office mandates, and unmanageable work have complicated workplace **THRIVE.** As a result, more people are testing the job market, seeking more from their work lives -- autonomy, purpose and meaning, growth and development opportunities, and better work-life balance.

Career Crossroads Examples

In this workbook, you'll find three diverse career crossroads examples that illustrate various pathways and decisions. Use these personas to guide your own reflections and choices as you *Design Your THRIVE.*

LEADERLESS LAYLAH

Leaderless Laylah is a 30-year-old information systems analyst. She has been a primary player for her previous leader, keeping projects on track. She isn't well known outside the team since her boss was the face of her work. Inside the team, she has been labeled a "teacher's pet" because others felt she received preferred treatment from the boss. Laylah faces challenges with the number and strength of her relationships and network since her previous leader was the active relationship builder. This has left Laylah somewhat isolated and wary of changes a new leader may bring.

Laylah is anxious and wants to maintain her successful track record while adapting to new circumstances as a new leader is selected. She recognizes she is experiencing a career crossroads and knows it's time to thoughtfully consider her path, purpose, and journey.

STUCK SHANDA

Shanda is a mid-career professional who, after six years in the same role, is feeling stuck and unfulfilled. While she once enjoyed the challenges and sense of accomplishment, she now finds herself trapped in a monotonous routine, working long hours without satisfaction.

Torn between the familiarity of her current job and the desire for something more meaningful, Shanda recognizes the need for change or potentially a new career path but is unsure of the next steps. Eager for clarity and guidance, she wants to evaluate her skills, interests, and values to make informed decisions about her future.

ASPIRING ALFREDO

Alfredo has been in the workforce just a few years. He is determined and seeks guidance, direction, and learning to elevate his skills, performance, and confidence. Eager to excel in his chosen field, he is looking for anything to jumpstart his progress. It's been difficult for Alfredo to build relationships since he works from home a few days per week.

Alfredo values continuous learning and seeks out resources and training programs to enhance his knowledge. He knows he is capable of more, but others haven't recognized his skills or provided more direction or guidance.

WHAT'S NEXT FOR YOU?

Tenets for **Design Your THRIVE** program:

Your path - You are the decision-maker

Your purpose - You define how you want to contribute and the impact you want to make

Your journey - You evolve a career on your terms, leveraging jobs, education, and experiences for your **THRIVE**

CAREER **THRIVE** TIPS

Recognize the Continuum
Remember that your career exists on a continuum with ebbs and flows based on your priorities and circumstances. This review process requires regular updates. The good news is that your ability to evaluate your **THRIVE** will grow as you gain more experience.

Manage Expectations
Expectations can be the killer of joy. Don't let unreasonable expectations, whether your own or others', define your career **THRIVE**. Allow yourself to be curious, open to ideas and alternate paths.

Focus Beyond Titles
It can be easy to chase titles, assuming they're the only way to job satisfaction, **THRIVE**, and success. However, a more effective approach involves asking yourself: What actions can I take today that will open greater opportunities tomorrow?

Develop Intrapersonal and Interpersonal Skills
Recognize the critical importance of intrapersonal and interpersonal skills in your career progression. Take time to develop these.

Increase Your Value
You expand your opportunities as you increase your value in an organization through high-quality performance, the opportunities you've accelerated, and the problems you've solved. Don't lose sight of the organization's needs in exchange for work.

Nurture Professional Relationships
Your work relationships and professional networks need constant care. Given the high leader and employee turnover rate in organizations, your key supporters and sponsors could disappear overnight.

Choose Your Adventure, Navigate Your Journey, and THRIVE

Dive into the content, assessments, and reflection questions in this workbook to guide your career crossroads path. The book is structured into five sections: Intention, Trust & Relationships, Growth & Development, Career Exploration, and *Design Your THRIVE* Road Map. Each section offers a variety of tools and resources.

Start with the Intention section to evaluate your elements of **THRIVE** at work, as it informs the Trust & Relationships, Growth & Development, and Career Exploration sections.

Set aside at least 60 minutes of focused time to complete each of the five sections.

Investing time to become more intentional about your career crossroads will make you more informed and better prepared to *Design Your THRIVE*, creating the conditions for personal growth, improved contribution, deeper connection, meaningful impact, and fulfillment in your job and career.

COMPILE YOUR ROAD MAP NOW

INTENTION

CAREER CROSSROADS

EDITION

INTENTION

PAUSE AND REFLECTION ARE SUPERPOWERS DURING
CAREER CROSSROADS

You will experience a career crossroads at some point. It could be deciding on your first or next job, getting a new leader, or perhaps experiencing a career quake— being laid off or fired, or encountering business financial problems or legal issues. Career crossroads are pivotal moments in your professional journey -- times for reflection, evaluation, and decision-making. Your choices at these junctures can impact future opportunities and fulfillment.

During these times, **intention becomes your compass**—a deliberate and purposeful approach to decision-making. It's about making choices that align your vision and values for your career and life rather than simply reacting to external circumstances or what others expect of you. Recognizing when you are at a crossroads can be challenging, and it may be even harder to pause and reflect, especially when anxiety and stress take hold or when you feel the need to prove your value.

Intention sets the direction - propelling your path, framing your purpose, and creating the space and license for your journey.

INTENTION

To **Design Your THRIVE**, you must first understand your current conditions and how they impact your **THRIVE** and fulfillment.

Research has shown that the following elements impact career and job satisfaction:

Purpose - Impact
When do you feel most fulfilled by your work? Does it align with your personal values and allow for a meaningful impact?

Your Organization - Leader
How well do you align with your organization's mission and values? What's your connection with your leader? Their engagement, support, and development of you matter.

Work Culture - Sense of Belonging
Do you feel appreciated and included? Is there room for your input and feedback? Do you feel like you belong and are part of the group?

Friends at Work
Trusting relationships are crucial. Do you have colleagues who support you?

Mentors- Sponsors
Are there individuals who guide and advise you or who use their influence to help advance your career?

Maximize Potential
Is your work challenging enough to maximize your strengths and skills?

Learning-Growth
Are there opportunities for you to learn and grow? Are you being challenged in ways that prepare you for future opportunities -- planned learning, stretch assignments, and coaching?

Pay-Benefits
Does your pay and benefits reflect your work? Does your work style—whether in-person, hybrid, or remote—suit your needs?

Tasks-Responsibilities
How do you feel about the type of work you do, the level of responsibility and mastery of your job? Do you have autonomy in your role? What functions do you love and what don't you?

Stress-Life Balance
Is your work manageable? Do you have control over how you integrate work with your personal life? How is your personal well-being?

The Intention section offers a variety of reflection activities that consider how you **THRIVE** in current or previous jobs. Reflect on the additional questions to provide direction to **Design Your THRIVE** — your path, purpose, and journey.

EVALUATE CAREER CROSSROADS

Reflect on the following questions to evaluate the motivations behind your decision to evaluate your job or career status.

Why are you at a career crossroads?

What do you hope to accomplish as part of this *Design Your THRIVE* evaluation?

What has been the impact of this crossroads on you personally? Describe your feelings, motivation, work performance as examples.

How high of a priority is this evaluation for you? Think of the commitment level you want to apply to these activities based on what you want to accomplish.

The next few pages of activities allow you to evaluate what you require to **THRIVE** in a job. You can evaluate your current job, what might be important in a new job, or the conditions of previous jobs that could provide current insight. Repeat as necessary for different jobs. Just be clear on what you are evaluating.

JOB THRIVE MAP

Evaluate your **THRIVE map** for a current or previous job(s).

Rate your level of fulfillment for each section on a scale of 1 to 10, with 1 being very dissatisfied and 10 being very satisfied with your job. Mark a line across each section to represent the score out of 10 you would give yourself. Refer to page 13 for the definitions of each category. **Repeat as necessary for previous jobs or future roles.**

Connect the lines to see your Job **THRIVE** Map like the one in the lower right-hand corner.

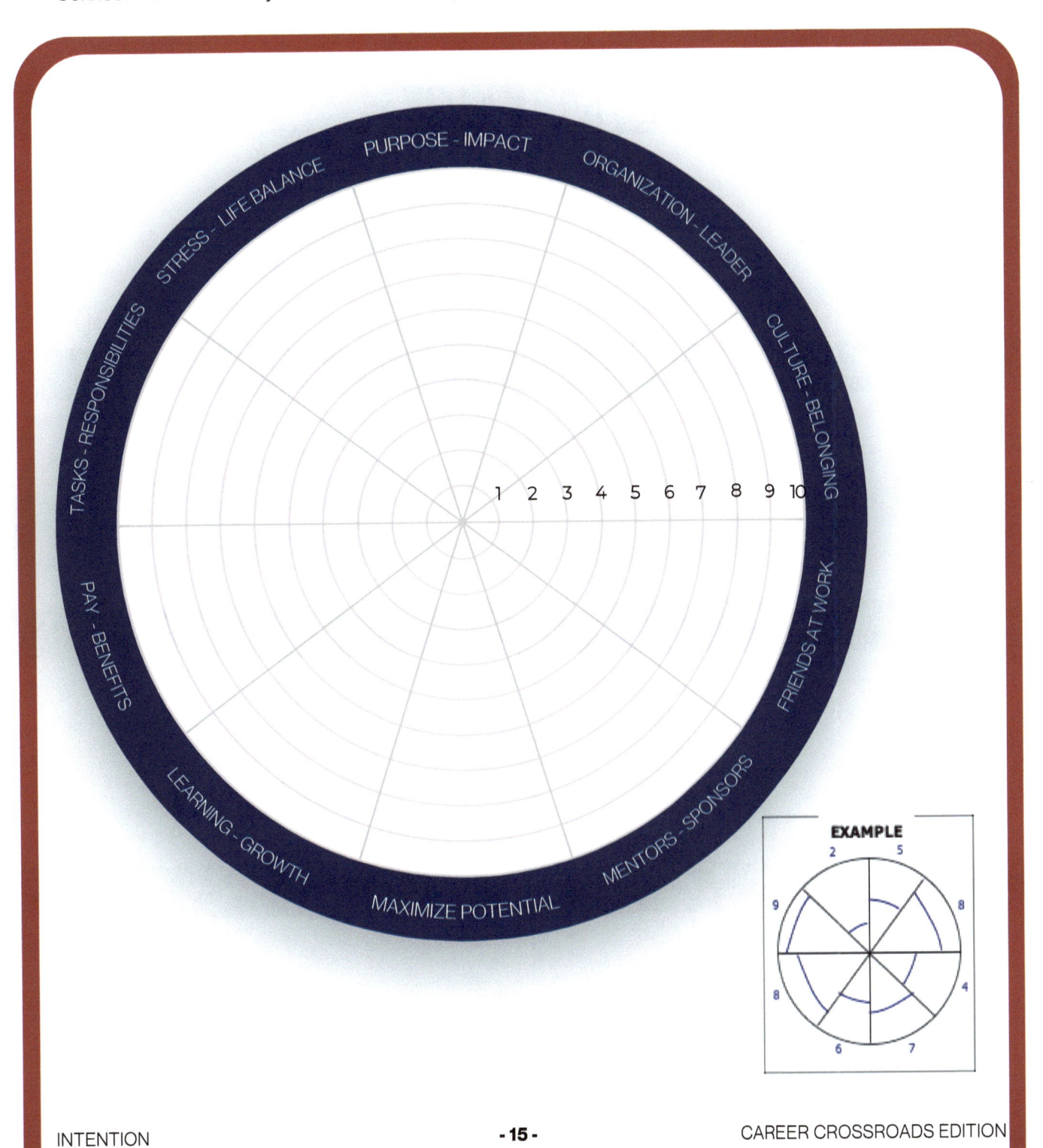

JOB **THRIVE** MAP

To learn more, consider each area on the wheel and write down a short statement that describes what a score of 10 would look like for each area. Or what a 10 might look like for you in a new role. Then think about the goals and the next steps you'll need to take to get to a 10 rating.

PURPOSE - IMPACT	ORGANIZATION - LEADER

CULTURE - BELONGING	FRIENDS AT WORK

MENTORS - SPONSORS	MAXIMIZE POTENTIAL

LEARNING - GROWTH	PAY - BENEFITS

TASKS - RESPONSIBILITIES	STRESS - LIFE BALANCE

JOB **THRIVE** CONSIDERATIONS

Reflecting on your **THRIVE** Map, answer the following questions to determine how you currently feel about these areas at work or in planning for a new role.

What did you learn about your current/previous job or yourself while reviewing your job **THRIVE** map(s)?

What are your 3 priorities from the **THRIVE** map for this job or your career development? What is most important right now or in the future?

What tactics or strategies might have the most impact on your job or career development? Consider the needs of both today and the future such as a change in full time or part time work, a side hustle, move to a new location, or new career interests.

What is your impact on the **THRIVE** map scoring?

What is your mindset? How committed have you been to the position, organization, or team? How have you sought out experiences to support your growth and learning? How have you built relationships? What is the impact of your expectations on your **THRIVE**? ***Designing Your THRIVE*** *begins with you and identifying the behaviors that complement your* **THRIVE**.

WHAT YOU'VE LEARNED ABOUT YOU

Use this worksheet to reflect on what makes you, you. These questions provide more context from your core beliefs, passions, performance, and previous experiences. This reflection can help you connect your past to the present and the evolving you.

YOUR CORE

Consider your values. How do your values impact your career choices?

_____
_____
_____
_____

What are your passions or interests? How do these factor in your career and job choices?

_____
_____
_____

What is the difference you make in the world or want to make through your career?

_____
_____
_____
_____

STRENGTHS AND SKILLS

What are your strengths and skills? What skills do others routinely compliment you on?

_____
_____
_____
_____

What skills or activities do you love or give you energy? When have you experienced flow at work?

_____
_____
_____

What knowledge or skills are evolving interests for you? Why is this important in career or job planning?

_____
_____
_____
_____

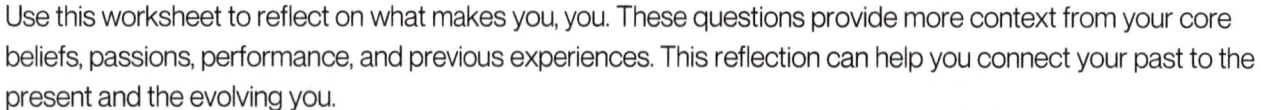

SUCCESS STORIES

Describe how you were able to use your skills for an assignment that added significant value to the outcome.

_____
_____
_____

What opportunities have you accelerated, and what problems have you solved in previous jobs? How did you make a difference?

_____
_____
_____

What became better because you participated? What is important to consider from your success stories?

_____
_____
_____

LESSONS LEARNED

When have you struggled? What were the circumstances? What did you learn?

_____
_____
_____

What were you able to overcome or tackle? When did a challenge motivate you? What did you learn?

_____
_____
_____

What things have held you back from being your best self at work? What did you learn?

_____
_____
_____

CAREER CONSIDERATIONS

Reflect on these additional questions, if you have broader career experience.

How satisfied are you with the evolution of your career - the jobs, experiences, learning, and related work? What is important to consider for this crossroads?

What accomplishments in your career or across various jobs are you most proud of? How have these achievements influenced your ability to **THRIVE**?

What did you learn if you evaluated more than one job or experience? What was the same or what was different and why?

Are you on the right path, purpose, or journey? If so, why. If not, why?

INTENTION

What is most important for you as you address your career crossroads?

Your current role, plan for career advancement - same or related field, pivot to new industry, plan for future needs, or begin career exploration? **Get specific -- consider your priorities. What is most important for you right now, in the near future, or to prepare for future needs?**

What are some specific strategies or tactics you might use to ***Design Your THRIVE?*** Recognize how feedback from your trusted relationships can help you view your **THRIVE** from different perspectives.

INTENTION
Review our career crossroads sample personas to see how they have evaluated their intention section.

DESIGN YOUR THRIVE - LEADERLESS LAYLAH'S REFLECTION AND PRIORITIES

- Laylah recognizes she is at a career crossroads and wants to have a positive transition with the new leader. She also recognizes that her quality work hasn't been widely known in the organization since her previous boss took the spotlight.

- It might also be time to evaluate her next career steps. Completing the **job THRIVE map** can identify key priorities for her work life. This will help prepare her for conversations with her new boss about her development. Perhaps her new leader could be a better mentor and advocate.

- Completing the **What You've Learned About You** worksheet will also help her qualify her experiences to date.

DESIGN YOUR THRIVE - STUCK SHANDA'S REFLECTION AND PRIORITIES

- Shanda recognizes that she is at a career crossroads - that fork in the road moment, does she stay, go, or grow?

- It is time to evaluate her career priorities. Completing the **job THRIVE map** can identify key priorities for her work life. This is also an opportunity to learn more about what she enjoys, what fulfills her, or what she feels she is missing.

- Shanda should dig deeper into her answers to the **Career Considerations** and **What You've Learned About You** questions. What have been motivators in the past and how can she translate this reflection for her roadmap?

DESIGN YOUR THRIVE - ASPIRING ALFREDO'S REFLECTION AND PRIORITIES

- Alfredo recognizes that he is at a career crossroads. He wants to grow and develop but is unsure of the best way to proceed.

- Completing the **job THRIVE map** can identify key priorities for his work life. This will help prepare him for conversations with his boss about his development and work needs.

INTENTION	notes, brainstorming & REFLECTION

TRUST & RELATIONSHIPS

CAREER CROSSROADS
EDITION

TRUST & RELATIONSHIPS

DURING CAREER CROSSROADS, LEAN INTO TRUST, RELATIONSHIPS, AND NETWORKS

In today's dynamic professional landscape, success hinges on trust, both earned and given. Extensive research underscores the pivotal role of TRUST, RELATIONSHIPS, and NETWORKS in fostering personal growth, job satisfaction, career trajectory, resilience, and overall career **THRIVE.**

Trust is not just a concept; it's your **career currency**—a mutual exchange of support, mentorship, guidance, and sponsorship. Your relationships inform your travel partners, their actions, and support for your journey.

When you invest in others, they often reciprocate, creating a powerful cycle of mutual growth and support. However, genuine trust requires ongoing cultivation, not merely collecting LinkedIn® connections like baseball cards. Digital technology and remote work have **weakened the number and strength of individual relationships.** Achieving transformational career **THRIVE** results demands a sustained effort to build and extend trust and connections.

TRUST DYNAMICS

Design Your THRIVE is built on **Trust Dynamics** and the 5 Cs of trust: Character, Connection, Competence, Courage, and Consistency. These domains outline how individuals earn and extend trust, fortifying the strength of relationships. Trust Dynamics also establishes your brand and reputation -- how others perceive and value you.

PROFESSIONAL NETWORKS are lifelines and catalysts during career crossroads. Prominent leadership researchers, Ibarra and Hunter, outline three critical networks—personal, operational, and strategic—that form the backbone of career success and resilience.

- **Personal Networks**: individuals with whom you have built a common personal relationship over time. They are interested in your success, growth, and development.

- **Operational Network**s: individuals whose work intersects with yours. Use these relationships to strengthen job-specific work performance.

- **Strategic Networks**: individuals who can extend your reach because of their influence. They are vital sponsors, influencers, or partners who can open a door, extend an invitation, offer an opportunity, or help you navigate career politics.

Mutual trust and strong, supportive relationships and networks can transform career crossroads moments.

TRUST DYNAMICS

Build your brand and reputation. Expand your resilience, value, networks, and impact using the 5 C's of Trust Dynamics.

CHARACTER
Exhibit high morals, honesty, integrity, and positive work ethic

CONNECTION
Build positive relationships with people and help shape success for others

COMPETENCE
Demonstrate proficiency and expertise in role

COURAGE
Willingness to take action, handle challenge, and be vulnerable

CONSISTENCY
Display consistency in behaviors and actions each day

trust

Julie Jones
Trust Metric© 2020, 2024

TRUST DYNAMICS ASSESSMENT

Relationships and networks are founded based on trust. Use the following worksheets to assess how well you demonstrate the behaviors of the 5 Cs of Trust (Trust Metric ©2020, 2024 Julie Jones). Those who have both earned and given trust are more resilient, more likely to **THRIVE** at work, and better equipped to navigate career crossroads.

For the behaviors noted for each category below, rate how well you demonstrate the behaviors where ten is always demonstrated, five is learning the skill, and one is not demonstrated or has no experience. Create a summary score for each category on the right side of the category. Identify your strengths and opportunities.

Character

exhibit high morals, honesty, integrity, and a strong work ethic

- Do more than is expected
- Proactive, take initiative, self-directed
- Actions match those expected from others
- Keep promises made to others
- Honest and truthful with others
- Adhere to the values and ethics of the organization
- Put the needs of others and the organization ahead of personal gain
- Accountable for work

How well have you earned trust in CHARACTER behaviors from others?

Strengths:

Opportunities:

Connection

build positive relationships, collaborate, communicate effectively, manage emotion productively, advocate and support others

- Build, nurture, and sustain positive relationships even in challenging situations
- Recognize and reward other's contributions and let others shine
- Demonstrate respect, kindness, and compassion
- Listen to other's ideas, perspectives, and concerns
- Welcome and include others and accept difference
- Keep others informed and communicate so that others understand
- Manage emotions productively
- Mentor others - Invest in people and their potential
- Advocate for others, supporting their job and career growth

How well have you earned trust in CONNECTION behaviors from others?

How well have you given trust in CONNECTION behaviors to others?

Strengths:

Opportunities:

Competence

demonstrate understanding and expertise, lifelong learner – grow and evolve behaviors and skills, prepare others for their roles

- Others are confident in your abilities and competence
- Demonstrate sound judgment
- Plan for and seek out learning opportunities to grow skills and invest in your development
- Seek out and apply feedback from others to improve
- Work to make things better
- Successfully navigate electronic technology for your needs
- Solve problems, provide solutions
- Learn and adapt to changing circumstances and needs
- Facilitate and support expertise learning for others

How well have you earned trust in COMPETENCE behaviors from others?

How well have you given trust in COMPETENCE behaviors to others?

Strengths:

Opportunities:

Courage

demonstrate strength in the face of adversity, courage to handle difficult tasks, willingness to show vulnerability

- Do the right thing even when it is hard or when others aren't
- Use your voice to make a positive difference
- Can voice an opinion different from the group
- Demonstrate grit and perseverance in challenging situations as needed
- Accept change and view it as an opportunity instead of a burden
- Can make tough decisions when necessary
- When appropriate, demonstrate vulnerability to promote teamwork and personal growth

How well have you earned trust in COURAGE behaviors from others?

Strengths:

Opportunities:

Consistency

constancy in performance day to day, equitable treatment of others

- Consistently perform and deliver high quality work and outcomes each day
- Fair and consistent in interactions with others
- Demonstrate consistency in behaviors, emotions, and actions each day

How well have you earned trust in CONSISTENCY behaviors from others?

Strengths:

Opportunities:

HOW STRONG ARE YOUR PROFESSIONAL NETWORKS?

It's not just about who you know; it's about their willingness to support, guide, or sponsor you during a career crossroads. These individuals could be in your personal, operational, or strategic networks. The strength of the relationship will directly correlate with the support, guidance, or sponsorship they would be willing to provide on your behalf. Remember, never burn bridges, as you never know when a previous relationship could open a future door for you.

DETERMINING THE STRENGTH OF A RELATIONSHIP

Weak

These individuals may be a common acquaintance or casual contact, someone with whom you have had a previous history in work, school, or other areas. Perhaps these individuals have fallen off your radar over time. Consider which individuals from this category can provide support during your career crossroads. How might you reinvest in these relationships to strengthen them?

Moderate

These individuals have had a more recent working or shared purpose history. There is likely some common ground connecting you, and you have built a level of support with them. Identify which individuals from this category can support you during this crossroads. How can you reinforce and maintain these connections?

Strong

These individuals have had consistent, positive experiences and interactions with you. You have earned their trust, and you extend trust to them. You value their opinion and guidance, and because of mutual trust, they can challenge you without harming the relationship. They fill roles like mentors, coaches, colleagues, peers, family, or friends. You feel comfortable reaching out to these individuals during career crossroads. Which individuals can support you during this career crossroads? How can you actively engage and involve them?

Robust

These individuals are shining stars in your network—they value you, believe in you, want the best for you, and have personally invested in your success. They may be few, but mighty! They will expend more time and effort to help you navigate career crossroads. What role can they best fill for you during this career crossroads—coach, counselor, sponsor, or other? How can you leverage their support effectively?

PROFESSIONAL NETWORKS ASSESSMENT

In the sections below, build your professional network list, identify the strength of the relationship, and the potential role they can fill for this career crossroads consideration. Narrow your list to those you might have the biggest impact for this crossroads need.

PERSONAL NETWORK

OPERATIONAL NETWORK

STRATEGIC NETWORK

OTHER INDIVIDUALS

TRUST DYNAMICS AND NETWORK STRENGTH

Evaluate the 5 C's of Trust Dynamics and the three networks— personal, operational, and strategic—on a scale of 1 to 10, where 10 is the highest score.

TRUST & RELATIONSHIPS

Reflect on these additional questions to summarize the information from your trust & relationships worksheets.

What did you learn from these trust and relationships exercises?

What are one or two opportunities to positively enhance your trust dynamics? What could have the most significant impact? **It is also powerful to solicit feedback from others about your Trust Dynamics so you can consider others' perspectives.**

What did you learn from your professional networks assessment? What support might you need from your networks to navigate this crossroads? Is your network ready and able to support your need currently? If not, what might you need to do?

CAREER CROSSROADS EXAMPLES

TRUST & RELATIONSHIPS

Review our career crossroads sample personas to see how they have evaluated their trust & relationships section.

DESIGN YOUR THRIVE - LEADERLESS LAYLAH'S REFLECTION AND PRIORITIES

- Laylah can complete the **professional networks** assessment and seek input from others on how she can strengthen her relationships with them. She should prioritize operational networks since these might be lacking.

- She can evaluate her **trust dynamics** and learn ways that she can extend trust to others as a way to build relationships.

- She might also **volunteer for assignments** to help her establish relationships with those outside her work team.

DESIGN YOUR THRIVE - STUCK SHANDA'S REFLECTION AND PRIORITIES

- Shanda can complete the **professional networks assessment** and identify people who can provide career exploration guidance or support. This activity will help Shanda create her personal career collective. She must get specific when she works with her network on how they can help.

- She can also identify others outside her network who can also provide direction.

DESIGN YOUR THRIVE - ASPIRING ALFREDO'S REFLECTION AND PRIORITIES

- Alfredo can complete the **trust dynamics assessment.** This is a great tool for early career employees, helping them establish their trust presence, both earned and extended. Trust becomes the framework for building and strengthening relationships.

- He can complete the **professional networks assessment** and seek input from his leader or peers, identifying people who can support his development. He should prioritize operational networks since these can significantly affect his growth, performance and impact .

- He can call upon his **personal networks** to provide guidance for learning and skill development. Alfredo is creating his learning collective, those willing to support him in his skill development.

- He should **prioritize building relationships** while in the workplace or working remotely. Prioritizing time with people helps create his presence. Seeking ways to partner with or help others in their role— extending trust to others or giving back—makes a difference. He can also **volunteer for assignments or investigate employee groups** available in his company.

TRUST & RELATIONSHIPS

notes, brainstorming & REFLECTION

GROWTH & DEVELOPMENT

CAREE**R**
CROSS**R**OADS
EDITION

GROWTH & DEVELOPMENT

EMBRACE LEARNING AS A COMPETITIVE ADVANTAGE DURING CAREER CROSSROADS

The pace of change in the professional landscape is accelerating. Technological advancements and market disruptions are constant, making what you know today obsolete within a few years. Success in the future hinges not solely on what you know today but also on your ability to continuously learn, adapt, and evolve to meet evolving workplace demands.

According to Dictionary.com, learning is defined as 'the acquisition of knowledge or skills through experience, study, or by being taught.' This broad definition intentionally opens many pathways for skill enhancement, job exploration, or career growth. Learning serves as the catalyst, propelling you past 'stuck' and other career crossroads moments. Curiosity, growth, and possibility are powerful motivators for learning and exploring.

Satya Nadella, the CEO of Microsoft, aptly remarked, *'Ultimately, the learn-it-all will always do better than the know-it-all.'* Committing to lifelong learning opens doors and creates additional opportunities, offering the potential for shifts and pivots in your journey.

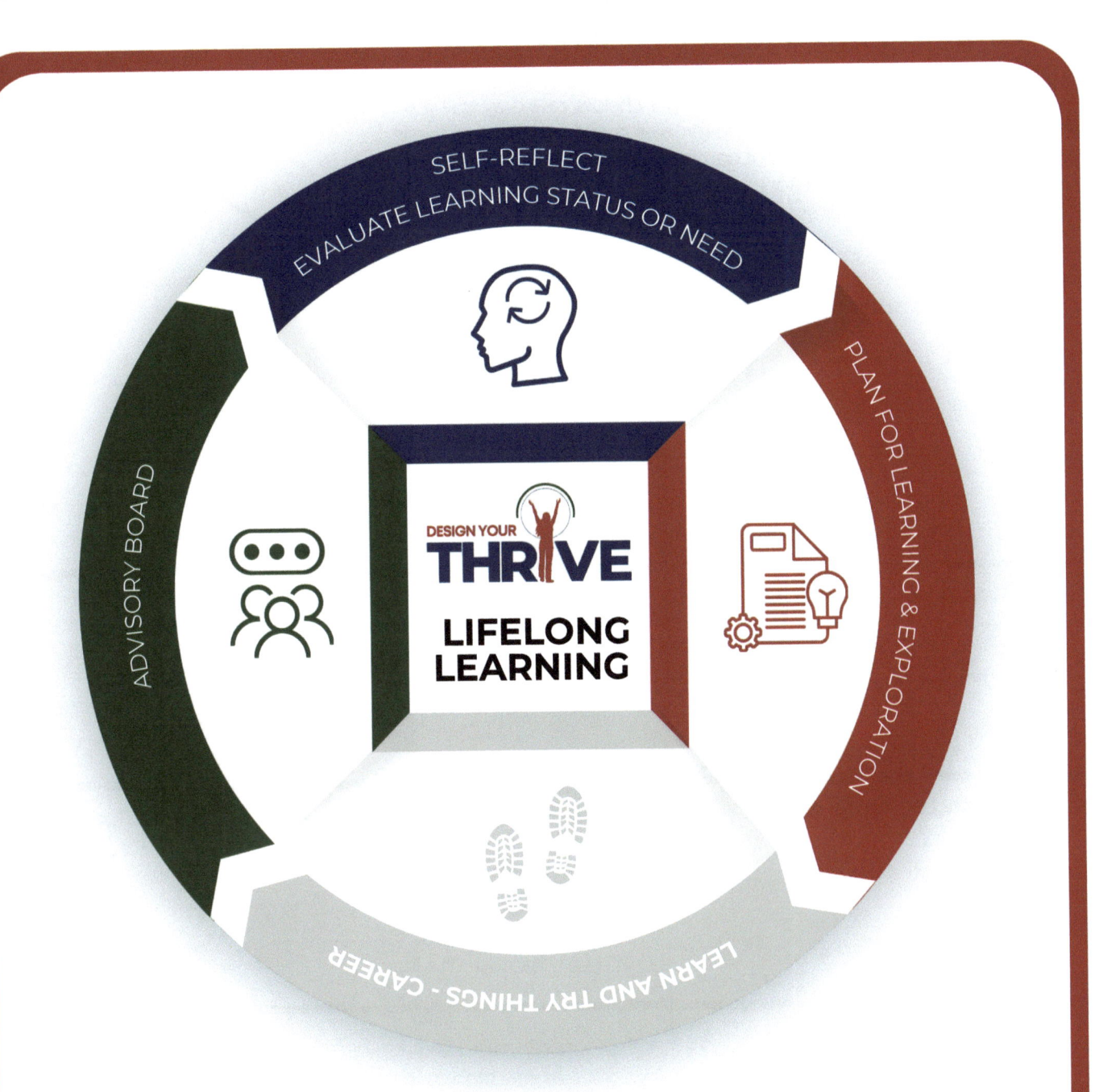

Design Your THRIVE considers lifelong learning a foundational element of Growth & Development. Extensive research consistently reinforces learning as a high-priority skill for current and future success. The process of learning, driven by curiosity, also fuels career exploration.

Learning as a skill is not just about gaining new knowledge. It goes one step further, beyond what you must know, and focuses on how well you prepare for learning, learn, and then apply the learning. Setting the stage for learning describes your **capacity** for learning. Complete the learning inventory assessment on the following page to evaluate your **capacity** for learning.

LEARNING INVENTORY – CAPACITY FOR LEARNING

For the behaviors noted for each category below, rate how well you demonstrate the behaviors where ten is always demonstrated, five is learning the skill, and one is not demonstrated or has no experience. Create a summary score for each category on the left side of the category. Identify your strengths and opportunities.

Awareness and open mind

Rating:

Strengths:

Opportunities:

- Open to new ideas, perspectives, and experiences
- Identify the need for learning and how to approach learning
- Comfortable with developing undefined processes
- Curious, ask questions and look for patterns in unrelated things
- Willingness to adapt to new situations
- Display a growth mindset – can accomplish learning
- Recognize own bias in thinking

Takes on risk with learning

Rating:

Strengths:

Opportunities:

- Acknowledge mistakes and learn from them
- Take on risk that new ideas and change brings
- Question status quo
- Take on learning when success isn't guaranteed

Effort and commitment

Rating:

Strengths:

Opportunities:

- Accept frustration that new learning can bring
- Patient and committed learner
- Practice skills
- Look deeper than the easy answer to grow skills
- Prioritize time for learning
- Internally motivated to learn

Evaluation and reflection

Rating:

Strengths:

Opportunities:

- Reflect on learning and evaluate progress in an intentional manner
- Create mental models to make sense of learning
- Review past experiences, learning successes, and failures for insights and apply to current or future needs
- Solicit and accept feedback as a growth tool
- Develop learning plan and track progress

Learning support team

Rating:

Strengths:

Opportunities:

- Solicit others to support learning – mentor, coach, colleague
- Stretch comfort zone – soliciting challenging feedback or opinions to grow skills
- Access people, tools, and resources to support growth and development

Knowledge, behaviors and skills describe your capabilities. **Design Your THRIVE** uses three broad domains for knowledge and skill capability consideration – Intrapersonal, Interpersonal, and Technical. A fourth domain, Career Exploration, describes career exploration and investigation processes.

Intrapersonal reflects behaviors and skills for personal growth and development and are inwardly focused.

Self-awareness, emotional intelligence, and adaptability are in demand skills.

Interpersonal reflects behaviors and skills that emphasize interactions and relationships with others.

Skills such as building relationships, empathy, and collaboration are noted as top needs by employers.

Technical skills refer to the job-specific and or industry-specific knowledge and skills required for current or future roles.

Career exploration - exploration and investigation processes you apply to learning and prototyping job or career development opportunities.

You bolster your **capability** when you learn and apply the learning for purpose.

Complete the Skills Inventory Assessments to evaluate your capabilities. For those at career pivots, you can also use the career exploration learning activities to evaluate your learning needs.

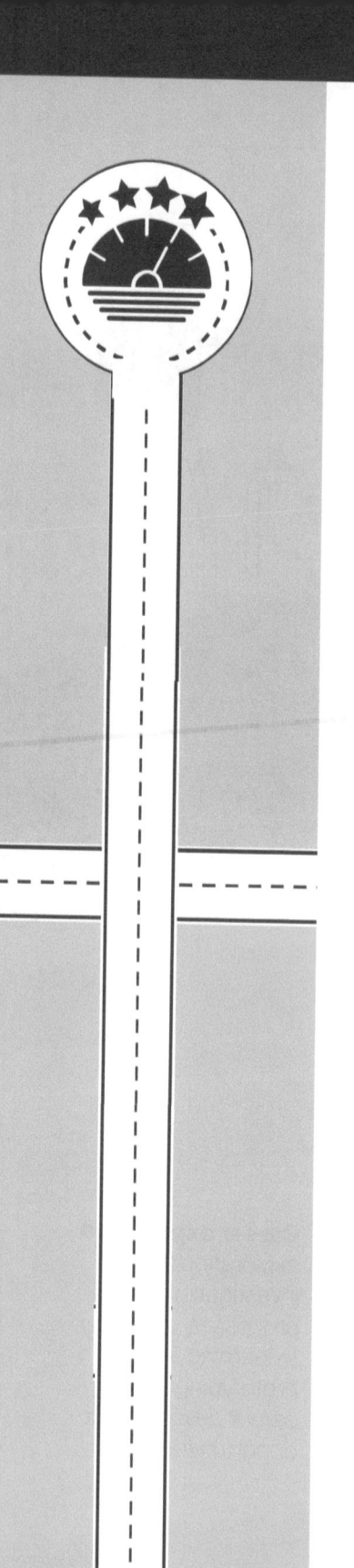

KNOWLEDGE, BEHAVIORS, AND SKILLS INVENTORY ASSESSMENTS

Please use the following directions to complete the knowledge and skills assessments on the following pages—**intrapersonal, interpersonal, and technical.** You can complete the skills inventory for your current role, for planning purposes, or for a future role or pivot. Just be clear with the job or role so that you understand the skill differences. Seek feedback on your performance, especially for high-priority skills.

You can do Google®, Indeed®, or LinkedIn® searches to review job skills. You can also refer to O*NET OnLine®, which lists occupational characteristics and worker requirements maintained by the U.S. Department of Labor.

1 Evaluate the **level of performance** in your current role or a skill required for a future role.

1 = Novice
- Limited ability to perform tasks independently.
- May have theoretical knowledge but lacks practical application.

2 = Beginner
- Can perform simple tasks with guidance.
- Understands basic concepts but struggles with complexity.
- Still developing confidence and efficiency in the skill.

3 = Advanced Beginner
- Demonstrates a solid grasp of concepts and techniques.
- Can handle routine problems and situations effectively.

4 = Proficient
- Can handle complex tasks and challenges effectively.
- Demonstrates a high level of confidence and efficiency.

5 = Expert
- Acts as a subject matter expert and mentor.
- Can handle highly complex and ambiguous situations with ease.
- Demonstrates innovation and thought leadership in the skill.

2 Prioritize your top 3 to 5 **development needs** for current or future roles. Check the box to the left of the skill name for your top 3 to 5 needs.

3 Record additional information in the Notes column, such as specific knowledge, behavior, skill strengths, or gaps to close.

Refer to the skill definition sheets on pages 44 to 46 to clarify the meaning for different knowledge, behaviors, and skill definitions.

INTRAPERSONAL KNOWLEDGE, BEHAVIORS, AND SKILLS INVENTORY ASSESSMENTS

INTRAPERSONAL KNOWLEDGE, BEHAVIORS, AND SKILLS are behaviors and skills that promote personal growth and development and are inwardly focused on you. Refer to the intrapersonal skill definition sheets on page 44..

KNOWLEDGE - SKILL	SKILLS CAPABILITY - CURRENT OR FUTURE ROLE (1 - 5)	EVALUATION AND NOTES	HIGHEST PRIORITIES
Self-awareness			☐
Learning capacity & capability			☐
Emotional intelligence			☐
Ethics & integrity			☐
Accountability			☐
Adaptability			☐
Resilience			☐
Critical thinking			☐
Creative thinking			☐
Systems thinking			☐
Problem solving			☐
Decision making			☐
Comprehension			☐
Writing			☐
Time management			☐

INTERPERSONAL KNOWLEDGE, BEHAVIORS, AND SKILLS are behaviors and skills that emphasize interactions and relationships with others. Refer to the interpersonal skill definition sheet on page 45.

HIGHEST PRIORITIES	KNOWLEDGE - SKILL	SKILLS CAPABILITY - CURRENT OR FUTURE ROLE (1 - 5)	EVALUATION AND NOTES
☐	Listening - Active listening		
☐	Communication		
☐	Social awareness		
☐	Trust - Building relationships		
☐	Navigating conflict		
☐	Negotiation		
☐	Influence		
☐	Coaching		
☐	Cultural humility		
☐	Inclusivity		
☐	Empathy		
☐	Service orientation		
☐	Partnership - Collaboration		
☐	Change		
☐	Delegation		

TECHNICAL KNOWLEDGE, BEHAVIORS, AND SKILLS refer to the job-specific and or industry-specific knowledge and skills required for current or future roles. Refer to the technical skills definitions on page 46..

KNOWLEDGE - SKILL	SKILLS CAPABILITY - CURRENT OR FUTURE ROLE (1 - 5)	EVALUATION AND NOTES	HIGHEST PRIORITIES
Digital fluency			☐
Data analytics			☐
Project management			☐
Financial acumen			☐
Strategy and planning			☐
Results orientation			☐
Job specific skills			☐
			☐
			☐
			☐
Industry specific skills			☐
			☐
			☐
			☐

INTRAPERSONAL KNOWLEDGE, BEHAVIORS AND SKILLS DEFINITIONS

Self-awareness: the ability to recognize and understand one's own thoughts, emotions, strengths, weaknesses, values, and motivations. (Neisser, U. (1995). Two perceptually given aspects of the self and their development. Developmental Review, 15(4), 403-427)

- The skill of self-awareness is to apply it to situations. This means comparing our awareness to the impression of others. Recognize if your ego becomes a barrier to learning or development.

Learning capacity and capability: the ability to learn and apply new knowledge to adapt to changing environment and expectations.

Emotional intelligence: the ability to navigate emotions to successfully build and maintain relationships.

Ethics and integrity: adhering to principles of honesty, fairness, and moral values, and acting with consistency, transparency, and accountability in personal and professional conduct. (Treviño, L. K., & Nelson, K. A. (2016). Managing business ethics: Straight talk about how to do it right (7th ed.). John Wiley & Sons)

Accountability: taking responsibility for one's actions, decisions, and commitments, and being responsible for the outcomes or results, whether positive or negative. (Bovens, M. A. (2007). Analysing and assessing accountability: A conceptual framework. European Law Journal, 13(4), 447-468)

Adaptability: the ability to adjust, change, or respond effectively to new circumstances, challenges, or environments, often involving flexibility and openness to change. (Martin, J. (2015). Organizational change: An action-oriented toolkit. Routledge)

Resilience: the ability to bounce back, recover, and cope with adversity, setbacks, or stressors, and maintain psychological well-being and performance. (Masten, A. S. (2001). Ordinary magic: Resilience processes in development. American Psychologist, 56(3), 227-238)

Critical thinking: the ability to analyze, evaluate, and interpret information objectively, logically, and systematically, often involving reasoning and problem-solving skills. (Facione, P. A. (2015). Critical thinking: What it is and why it counts (2015 update). Insight Assessment)

Creative thinking: the capacity to generate new ideas, solutions, or perspectives by thinking innovatively, imaginatively, and outside conventional boundaries. (Isaksen, S. G., Dorval, K. B., & Treffinger, D. J. (2000). Creative approaches to problem solving: A framework for change (2nd ed.). Sage Publications)

Systems thinking: the ability to understand complex systems, identifying patterns, relationships, and interconnections, and considering the broader context and implications. (Senge, P. M. (1994). The fifth discipline: The art & practice of the learning organization. Currency Doubleday)

Problem solving: the ability to identify, analyze, and resolve problems or challenges effectively, often involving critical thinking, creativity, and decision-making skills. (Jonassen, D. H. (2011). Learning to solve problems: A handbook for designing problem-solving learning environments. Routledge)

Decision making: the ability to evaluate options, assess consequences and risks, and choose the best course of action to achieve a goal or desired outcome. (Simon, H. A. (1979). Nobel Prize Lecture)

Comprehension: the ability to understand and interpret information or concepts, including reading, listening, and understanding ideas or instructions. (Mayer, R. E. (2009). Multimedia learning (2nd ed.). Cambridge University Press)

Writing: the ability to express ideas, thoughts, and information in written form, including clarity, coherence, and effective communication. (Graham, S., & Perin, D. (2007). Writing next: Effective strategies to improve writing of adolescents in middle and high schools. Alliance for Excellent Education)

Time management: the ability to organize, prioritize, and manage time efficiently and effectively to achieve goals, meet deadlines, and balance tasks and responsibilities. (Lakein, A. (1973). How to get control of your time and your life. P.H. Wyden)

Listening: the ability to pay attention to and process information to understand and show respect and interest for the speaker. (DeVito, J. A. (2021). Interpersonal Communication Book (15th ed.). Pearson)

Active listening: the ability to engage in a specific style of listening where the listener demonstrates understanding and engages with the speaker through verbal and nonverbal cues, such as paraphrasing, asking clarifying questions, and providing feedback. (Guffey, M. E., & Loewy, D. (2021). Essentials of Business Communication (12th ed.). Cengage Learning)

Communication: the ability to communicate, create common understanding, connection, and buy in through different types of communication – verbal, nonverbal, and written communication.

Social awareness: the ability to accurately understand the emotions, perspectives, and situations of others, as well as the ability to navigate social dynamics effectively. (Goleman, D. (2006). Social Intelligence: The New Science of Human Relationships. Bantam)

Trust-Building Relationships: the ability to establish trust to build and maintain relationships and networks that support performance, growth, and development. See Trust Dynamics.

Negotiation: the ability to engage in a communication process where two or more parties discuss and collaboratively reach an agreement on a shared outcome, demonstrating adeptness in compromise and problem-solving. (Lewicki, R. J., Barry, B., & Saunders, D. M. (2015). Negotiation: Readings, Exercises, and Cases (7th ed.). McGraw-Hill Education.)

Navigating conflict: the ability to successfully navigate and resolve conflicts —both those that are impair performance as well as those that stimulate growth and new ideas.

Influence: the ability to persuade, inspire, and propel others towards a vision, purpose, goal, or activity.

Cultural humility: the ability to demonstrate an attitude of openness, self-awareness, and willingness to learn from and engage with individuals from different cultural backgrounds, while recognizing and respecting their perspectives and experiences. (Tervalon, M., & Murray-García, J. (1998). Cultural humility versus cultural competence: A critical distinction in defining physician training outcomes in multicultural education. Journal of Health Care for the Poor and Underserved, 9(2), 117-125)

Inclusivity: the ability to accept and include individuals/groups and build respectful and open-minded dialogue.

Empathy: the ability to understand and share the feelings, thoughts, and experiences of others, often leading to compassionate and supportive interactions. (Davis, M. H. (1983). Measuring individual differences in empathy: Evidence for a multidimensional approach. Journal of Personality and Social Psychology, 44(1), 113-126)

Coaching: the ability to apply a planned coaching process using assessment, intentional learning, practice, and feedback to invest in people, their performance, and growth.

Service orientation: the ability to elevate the customer experience and consider customer needs when creating products and services.

Partnership and collaboration: the ability to work collaboratively with others towards a common goal or purpose. This includes building and maintaining mutually beneficial relationships, communicating openly and transparently, sharing responsibilities, resources, leveraging diverse perspectives and skills, and accomplishing shared objectives. (Thompson, L. L. (2020). Making the Team: A Guide for Managers (6th ed.). Pearson)

Change: the ability to plan, implement, and manage change including strategies to mitigate resistance and support others in transitions. (Cummings, T. G., & Worley, C. G. (2014). Organization Development and Change (10th ed.). Cengage Learning)

Delegation: the ability to entrust tasks, responsibilities, and decision-making authority to others while maintaining accountability for the outcomes. Assigns tasks based on skills and capabilities, empowers others to take ownership of their work, and provides necessary support and guidance. (Allen, D. (2021). Delegation & Supervision (2nd ed.). American College of Healthcare Executives)

TECHNICAL KNOWLEDGE, BEHAVIORS AND SKILLS DEFINITIONS

Digital fluency: the ability to effectively use digital technologies, tools, and platforms to communicate, collaborate, create, analyze data, and solve problems in a digital environment. (Beetham, H., & Sharpe, R. (2019). Digital Literacies: Principles and Practices (2nd ed.). Routledge)

Data analytics: the ability to capture, use, and apply data effectively and consistently for business decision making.

Project management: the ability to initiate, plan, execute, control, and close projects effectively and efficiently to achieve specific goals and meet predetermined success criteria within a specified timeframe and budget. (Schwalbe, K. (2021). Information Technology Project Management (9th ed.). engage Learning)

Financial acumen: the ability to interpret financial information to make informed decisions and contribute to the financial health and success of an organization. (Mayo, H. B., Shank, J. K., & Bernard, J. J. (2020). Basics of Budgeting and Financial Management (3rd ed.). Wiley)

Strategy and planning: the ability to connect operations, organization priorities, and knowledge of industry to craft and successfully implement vision and strategy to positively impact outcomes.

Results orientation: the ability to focus on achieving measurable outcomes, delivering high-quality work, meeting deadlines, and continuously improving performance to drive tangible and positive results for individuals, teams, and organizations. (Meyer, J. P., & Herscovitch, L. (2001). Commitment in the Workplace: Toward a General Model. Human Resource Management Review, 11(3), 299-326)

Job specific knowledge or skills: Add additional knowledge, behaviors or skills that are required for the individual to successfully perform their job or would be required future job.

Industry specific knowledge or skills: Add additional knowledge, behaviors or skills that are industry specific and provide the context and framework for individuals to successfully perform their job, or would be required for a future job, or career pivot. Industries group jobs with similar activities, products, or services. These might also include certifications or education required for certain jobs.

DEVELOPING SKILLS PATHWAY
PLANNING LEARNING

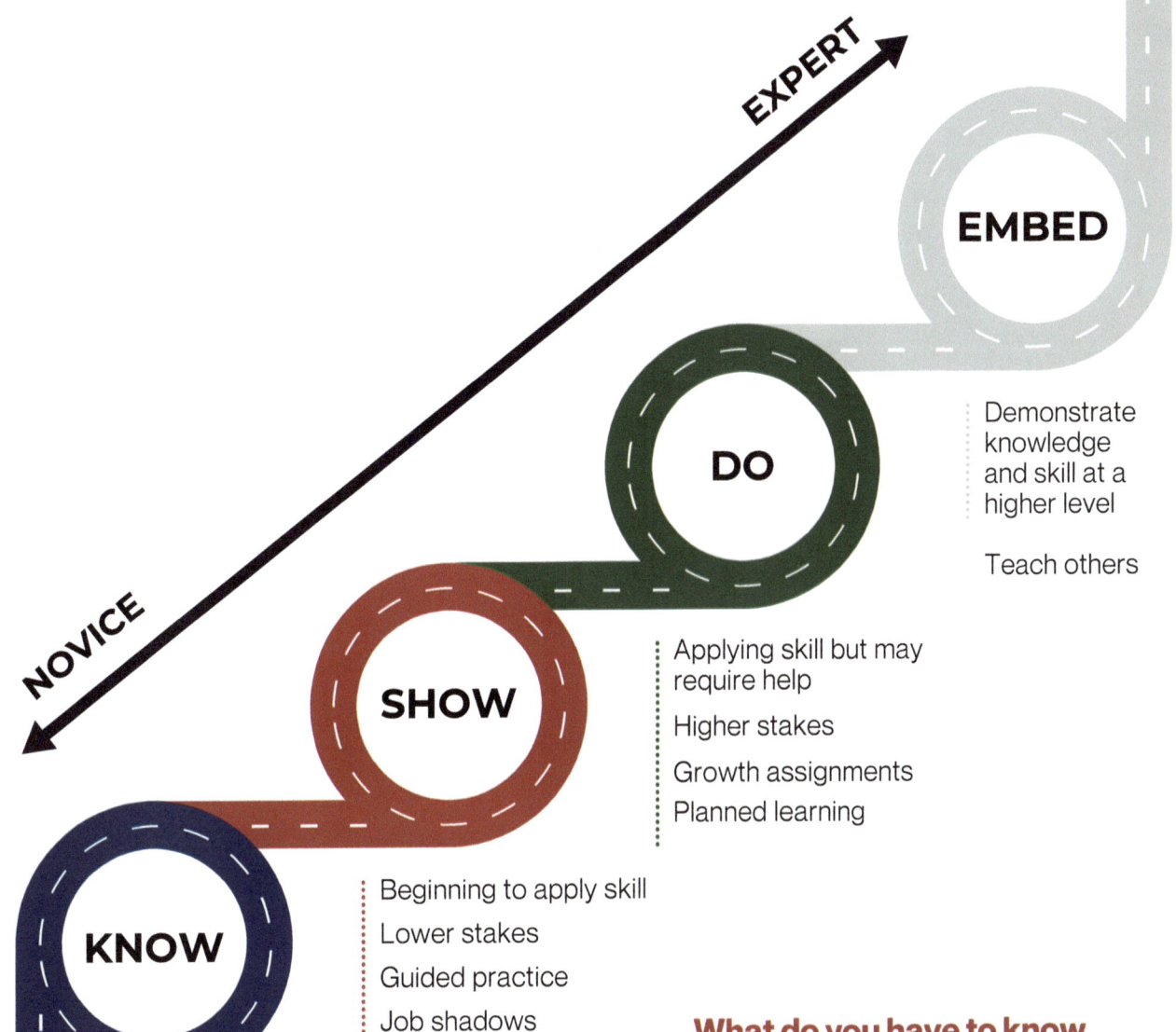

EXPERT

NOVICE

EMBED

Demonstrate knowledge and skill at a higher level

Teach others

DO

Applying skill but may require help

Higher stakes

Growth assignments

Planned learning

SHOW

Beginning to apply skill

Lower stakes

Guided practice

Job shadows

Interviews

KNOW

Have required knowledge

What do you have to know before you can do?

Taking time to learn the content and a framework for the skill will make mastering the skill easier. Note the different steps to sequence learning to move from novice to expert status.

YOUR IMPACT AND VALUE

As you assess your career path, remember it's not just about your skills. It's also about how you use them to make an impact and add value. Consistent, high-quality work builds your trust and value in an organization and strengthens your **THRIVE** story.

Use the questions below to synthesize the information from the knowledge and skill assessments, and explore ways you've turned your skills into meaningful results and impact.

What major accomplishments have you or a team made based on your unique contribution and skills? How has this contributed to your **THRIVE**?	
What opportunities have you accelerated in one of your roles? How did your skills or presence make a difference? Why did this matter for you?	
What problems did you solve using your skills and strengths? How did you use them to overcome challenges or obstacles? What was the impact on your motivation and **THRIVE**?	
How well have you met or exceeded job expectations and provided high-quality performance? Describe specific examples.	
How well have you engaged others as part of your performance? How aware are others of your performance or what is their perception of your skills?	

GROWTH & DEVELOPMENT MAP

Evaluate your capacity for learning from page 38 and skills capabilities on pages 41 – 43. Consider these elements – capacity, intrapersonal skills, interpersonal skills, and technical skills for the growth and development map. Record your assessment using a scale of 1 to 10, where 10 is the highest score for each of the four elements. Where are your strengths and what are your gaps?

GROWTH & DEVELOPMENT

Reflect on these additional questions to summarize the information from the growth & development worksheets.

What did you learn from these growth, development, and learning exercises?

What one or two opportunities can positively impact your learning capacity - awareness and open mind; risk of learning; effort and commitment; evaluation and reflection; learning support team? How might you do this and what support might you need?

What are the priority areas and needs for your skills development? How might you approach this learning? Who might be able to help? How will you evaluate success?

CAREER EXPLORATION LEARNING

Career exploration is like lifelong learning—an evolving journey where each new learning, experience, or job contributes to your self-awareness and understanding of where and how you **THRIVE**. Reflect on the questions in this section to help you navigate pivot points - first job, new career, or return to work. **You might not need to complete this inventory if you are satisfied with your current path, purpose, and journey.**

INTENTION - PAUSE AND REFLECTION STAGE

- What is important at this stage of your career?
- What are your values, interests, or passions driving career exploration?
- What do you want to address from your **THRIVE** map? Translate these **THRIVE** element considerations into job or career considerations and prioritize them.
- What are the outcomes you want to achieve from this career exploration?

- Are there things you can explore or do in your current job to enhance your **THRIVE** or future success?
- Complete job shadows or informational interviews to learn more
- Explore different organizations and their job postings - What interests you?
- Seek out volunteer organizations or internship opportunities to learn more, test drive skills, or grow skills
- Attend career fairs, workshops, or association meetings to learn from others
- Identify online resources like the *Occupational Outlook Handbook*, O*NET OnLine®, or other career exploration websites to learn about different professions, job duties, required skills, education, and salary expectations
- Follow industry-related blogs or individuals that interest you
- Identify career planning or crossroads books or podcasts that interest you

INVESTIGATION AND EVALUATION
- SYNTHESIZE INFORMATION AND LEARNING

- Summarize your strengths and skills from the previous exercises
- How can you leverage your previous experiences, jobs, and skills as a pivot for new roles?
- Evaluate your intention and **THRIVE** map needs compared to different jobs, careers, and work environments
- What types of roles may be a good fit for you at this career stage?
- What excited and interested you or takes advantage of your strengths and skills and will maximize your potential?
- What are my skill or education gaps?
- What challenges will help me grow?

PLAN

- What are your learning priorities - education, content, skills, and experiences that would best prepare you for a career crossroads transition?
- What are some specific strategies and timelines to achieve?

Rate your career exploration for the different stages -- intention, exploration, investigation, and plan where 1 is just starting, and 10 is well-informed. What are your opportunities to be more intentional with career exploration?

CAREER EXPLORATION

Complete this worksheet if you prioritized career exploration. Reflect on these additional questions to summarize the information from your career exploration worksheet.

What did you learn from these learning, skill, and career exploration exercises?

What one or two opportunities can positively impact your career exploration? Complete the career exploration plan later in this section to activate your ideas,

What are the priority areas and needs for your skills development? How might you approach this learning? Who might be able to help? How will you evaluate success?

CAREER EXPLORATION PLAN

Use this form to record your top 2 or 3 exploration and learning opportunities in each stage and track progress.

CAREER EXPLORATION STAGE	POTENTIAL ACTIVITIES, EXPERIENCES, LEARNING	NOTES FOR SCHEDULING ACTIVITIES AND POST EXPERIENCE FOLLOW UP	DATE TO REVIEW
INTENTION	• Values • Interests, passion • Purpose • **THRIVE** map elements • Strengths and skills		
EXPLORATION	• Review current job • Job shadows • Informational interviews • Other organizations and jobs • Volunteer or internship opportunities • Career fairs, workshops, or association meetings • Online resources • Industry blogs • Books or podcasts		
INVESTIGATION	• Summarize strengths and skills • Compare intention and **THRIVE** map for different jobs, careers, work environments • Types of roles for career stage • Maximize potential • Challenges you would like to tackle • Skill or education gaps • Synthesize information and learning		
PLAN	• Learning priorities – education, content, skills, and experiences		

CAREER CROSSROADS EXAMPLES

LEARNING & CAREER EXPLORATION

Review our career crossroads sample personas to see how they have evaluated their growth & development and career exploration sections.

DESIGN YOUR THRIVE - LEADERLESS LAYLAH'S REFLECTION AND PRIORITIES

- Laylah should complete the **knowledge, behaviors, and skills assessments** and connect these to her performance. She can also seek out feedback and additional opinions. These exercises will help her qualify and quantify her value, impact, and contribution.

- Laylah is confident she is in the right work industry but is unsure of additional career options based on her experiences. To learn more, she can complete the **career exploration worksheet.** This provides an intentional approach to provide her with more options if things change with the new leader.

- She can create a **career exploration plan** and link learning needs to knowledge and skills that could open additional pathways.

DESIGN YOUR THRIVE - STUCK SHANDA'S REFLECTION AND PRIORITIES

- Shanda can complete the **knowledge, behaviors, and skills assessments**, connecting these to her performance. She can seek out additional opinions. These exercises will help her qualify and quantify her value, impact, and contribution and can clarify the activities she enjoys.

- These assessments can also prepare her for conversations with her leader or her career collective, helping her decide whether to stay, go, or grow.

- She can become a career explorer by completing the **career exploration worksheet** and investigating career opportunities within her existing organization.

- Complete a **career exploration plan** and link learning needs to knowledge and skills that could open additional pathways.

DESIGN YOUR THRIVE - ASPIRING ALFREDO'S REFLECTION AND PRIORITIES

- Alfredo can complete the **knowledge, behaviors, and skills assessments** and connect these to his performance. He can also ask others for feedback. These exercises will help him qualify and quantify priority skills and development needs.

- He can create a **personal development plan** to support his growth and development. He can call upon his learning collective and engage them in his development journey. Prioritizing learning with others can also be a way to strengthen his relationships.

GROWTH & DEVELOPMENT CAREER EXPLORATION

notes, brainstorming & REFLECTION

DESIGN YOUR THRIVE ROAD MAP

Transfer your **THRIVE**, Trust & Relationships, Growth & Development, and Career Exploration maps to create a summary road map. Use the examples Leaderless Laylah, Stuck Shanda, and Aspiring Alfredo as guides.

SUMMARY REVIEW
INTENTION

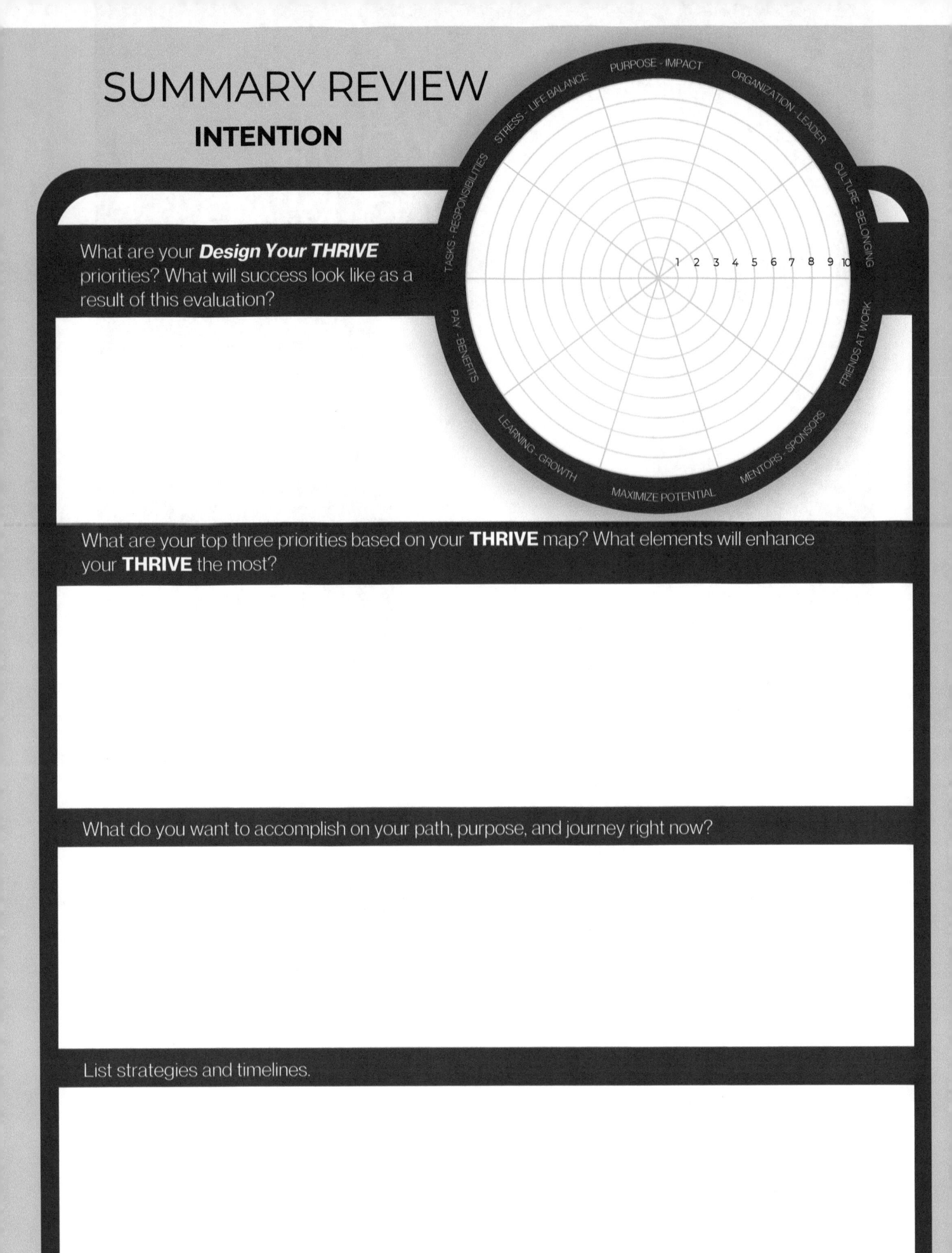

What are your **Design Your THRIVE** priorities? What will success look like as a result of this evaluation?

What are your top three priorities based on your **THRIVE** map? What elements will enhance your **THRIVE** the most?

What do you want to accomplish on your path, purpose, and journey right now?

List strategies and timelines.

SUMMARY REVIEW
TRUST & RELATIONSHIPS

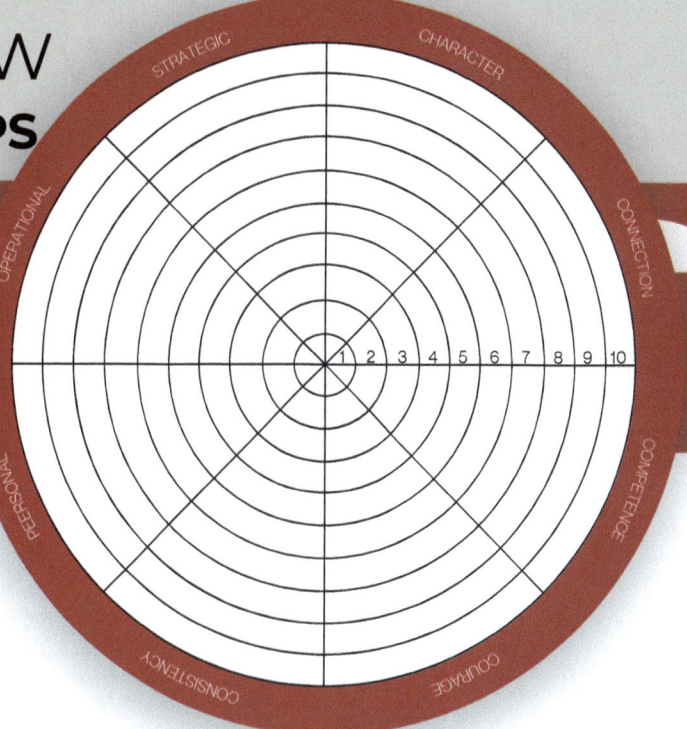

What are your top two or three opportunities to strengthen your trust dynamics, brand, or reputation? Identify strategies and timelines to address. Keep it simple.

What might you need to address in the strength of your networks to address your *Design Your THRIVE* needs? Be specific. Describe how you might measure success.

SUMMARY REVIEW
GROWTH & DEVELOPMENT

How well have you translated your skills, interests, **THRIVE** elements, and job considerations for your growth and development or career exploration needs? What else might you need to consider?

What are the priorities and timelines from your personal learning plan or career exploration plan?

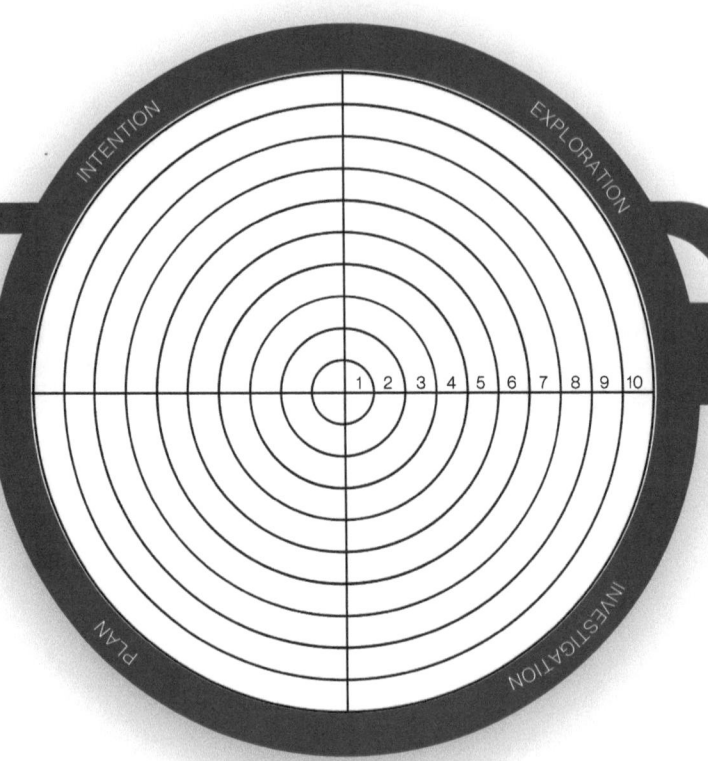

On the next page, translate your growth and development needs into a **DESIGN YOUR THRIVE** Development Plan. Allow yourself at least 60 minutes to thoughtfully consider your priorities, specific growth and development activities, and a timeline you can commit to.

The **DESIGN YOUR THRIVE** Development Plan serves several vital purposes:

- **Action Planning:** Provides clear steps to propel your growth and progress
- **Discussion Preparation:** Organizes your thoughts for productive conversations with mentors, colleagues, or friends, helping you to secure their support
- **Progress Tracking:** Functions as a dynamic tool to gauge your ongoing development and learning

DESIGN YOUR THRIVE DEVELOPMENT PLAN

Use this form to record your top 2 or 3 development opportunities from each section. Identify a date to review and track progress.

DATE _____

	SPECIFIC DEVELOPMENT ACTIVITIES	REVIEW/REFLECT – DO KNOWLEDGE, SKILLS AND/OR BEHAVIORS MATCH DESIRED GROWTH?	DATE TO REVIEW
INTENTION			

What Is Your Why?
Vision | Values | Path |
Purpose | Journey
Strengths | Passion |
Energy

THRIVE Map Elements
Purpose - Impact | Organization - Leader | Culture -
Belonging | Friends at Work | Mentors - Sponsors |
Maximize Potential | Learning - Growth | Pay - Benefits |
Tasks - Responsibilities | Stress - Life Balance

What Is Important To Accomplish?
Priorities for job or career development What is important right now or for the future?

Use this form to record your top 2 or 3 development opportunities from each section. Identify a date to review and track progress.

DATE _____

	SPECIFIC DEVELOPMENT ACTIVITIES	REVIEW/REFLECT – DO KNOWLEDGE, SKILLS AND/OR BEHAVIORS MATCH DESIRED GROWTH?	DATE TO REVIEW
TRUST & RELATIONSHIPS			

Trust Dynamics
Character | Connection | Competence | Courage | Consistency

Networks
Personal | Operational | Strategic
Mentors | Sponsors | Advocates

Social Awareness
Earned and given trust

Use this form to record your top 2 or 3 development opportunities from each section. Identify a date to review and track progress.

DATE _____

	SPECIFIC DEVELOPMENT ACTIVITIES	REVIEW/REFLECT – DO KNOWLEDGE, SKILLS AND/OR BEHAVIORS MATCH DESIRED GROWTH?	DATE TO REVIEW
LEARNING & CAREER DEVELOPMENT			

Intrapersonal Skills:
Accountability | Adaptability | Critical Thinking | Creative Thinking | Systems Thinking | Comprehension | Problem Solving | Decision Making | Emotional Intelligence | Ethics and Integrity | Learning Capacity and Capability | Resilience | Self-Awareness | Time Management | Writing

Interpersonal Skills:
Listening | Active Listening | Change | Coaching | Communication | Cultural Humility | Delegation | Empathy | Inclusivity | Influence | Motivation | Navigating Conflict | Negotiation | Partnership and Collaboration | Service Orientation | Social Awareness | Trust – Building Relationships

Technical Skills:
Data Analytics | Digital Fluency | Financial Acumen | Project Management | Results Orientation | Strategy and Planning | Include others specific for your needs

SUMMARY REFLECTION

How will you evaluate your success? What are some milestones or benchmarks you can use to track progress?

What support might you need to boost your motivation to continue?

DESIGN YOUR THRIVE PROGRESS UPDATE

In the sections below, update the progress of your **Design Your THRIVE** journey considering the questions in each box. Review and revise initially at 3 months, and every 6 months until you are more satisfied with your **THRIVE** or direction. Use these tools consistently throughout your career as you evaluate your path, purpose, and journey.

INTENTION

Review your **THRIVE** level at work using the **THRIVE Map**. What has changed?

_____
_____
_____
_____

What strategies worked to help you become more intentional in this process?

_____
_____
_____

What would you still like to do?

_____
_____
_____

TRUST & RELATIONSHIPS

How has your Trust Dynamics evolved over this review period? What has changed in earned and given trust?

_____
_____
_____
_____

What relationships and networks have changed?

_____
_____
_____

What would you still like to do?

_____
_____
_____

GROWTH, DEVELOPMENT, LEARNING & CAREER EXPLORATION

What were you able to accomplish with learning, skill development, or career exploration activities?

_____
_____
_____

What makes sense, still challenges you, or do you want to know more about?

_____
_____
_____

What are your updated priorities for learning and exploration?

_____
_____
_____

VALUE AND IMPACT

Evaluate value and impact for those in a current position. What is different or the same?

_____
_____
_____

What opportunities do you have to increase your value or impact?

_____
_____
_____

What specific strategies could you use in paid or unpaid roles, to advance your progress?

_____
_____
_____

KUDOS FOR INVESTING TIME IN
YOU!

SHIFT INTO DRIVE

During this process, you've planned a roadmap grounded in **intention.** You've identified your travel partners and opportunities to strengthen **trust** and ways to build your **YOU** team. You've evaluated **learning** or **career exploration** needs to evolve your skills based on your career roadmap.

Audrey Hepburn once famously said, "*Nothing is impossible; the word itself says, I'm possible.*"
This quote highlights the boundless potential that resides within you if you take action to *Design Your THRIVE.*

ROADMAP TIPS

No Right or Wrong Route
There is no right or wrong route – you might get lost, experience detours, or stay in the express lane. Embrace the concept of motion and continuous learning to keep evolving. As Robert Frost said in his poem, The Road Not Taken, *"I took the one less traveled by, And that has made all the difference."* Value your journey for the experiences that allow you to create a rich and deep atlas.

Match Your Speed to Your Goals
Match the speed of your crossroads journey to your desired outcomes. Take time where you can, seek support when you need to adjust your pace, and remember to embrace motion as a path forward.

Set Milestones and Find a Partner
Set milestones or destinations for your journey. Find an accountability partner to help keep you on track and support you.

Use Your Compass
Let your vision, values, and priorities guide your choices and help you **THRIVE**. As writer Alvin Toffler said, *"You've got to think about big things while you are doing small things so that all of the small things go in the right direction."*

Take Breaks and Refuel
Give yourself a layover when you need a break. Don't forget to enjoy the broader journey of life. Fuel your engine by identifying activities or opportunities that excite you, generate interest, spark new possibilities, or grow desired skills.

ABOUT THE AUTHOR

JULIE JONES

MS, RDN, LD, CPTD

For over three decades, Julie has led, taught, and collaborated with thousands of of individuals—employees, college students, clients, and colleagues alike—across dynamic roles as a leader, consultant, teacher, and mentor.

She directed the multi-hospital award-winning food and nutrition program at The Ohio State University Wexner Medical Center, and Julie was awarded the Silver Plate for Healthcare Foodservice. As the Director of Performance Learning at Ruck-Shockey Associates, she helps clients grow their leadership talent and align their priorities and programs for tangible business outcomes. Julie also teaches college students to embrace their capacity for learning and leadership in the Masters in Dietetics and Nutrition program at The Ohio State University.

Julie's career now spans talent development and she has become a Certified Professional in Talent Development.

Her experiences have taught her a fundamental truth: at the core of sustainable personal, team, and business success are people who **THRIVE** at work—driven by intention, bolstered by strong relationships and networks, and supported by leaders who cultivate trust, both earned and given, in an environment that promotes learning, growth, resilience, and contribution.

Julie's passion for empowering others led to the creation of ***Design Your THRIVE***, a resource born from research, real-life stories, and her professional experience. Through this work, she wants to inspire and equip others with the tools and resources to **THRIVE** at work.

"You do not just wake up and become the butterfly.
Growth is a **process**."

Rupi Kaur, *The Sun and Her Flowers*

Contact us at **learning@ruckshockey.com or** visit us at
www.learning.ruckshockey.com for
learning and development recommendations, additional
resources, or to work with us. .

Graphic Design : Agnes Manguiat